The Incredible Honeybee

A Layman's Reference Guide

by
T.J. Allen

First Edition: October 2015

Printed in the United States of America

ISBN: 978-0-9962922-0-7

To My Wife, Lynn and Kids, Jonathan, Seth, Lindsey, and Miranda; the five people who mean the world to me and, who put up with my varied and sometimes outrageous schemes to discover new things.

Table of Contents

Acknowledgements

Thanks to Kelley Beekeeping Company for the use of the various photographs from their website and, for the great customer service they have provided over the years.

All photographs with "KBC" at the bottom are used by permission from the Kelley Beekeeping Company website; www.kelleybees.com.

Thanks to my friends Trey and Teresa Hodges for their friendship and advice concerning this book and their wonderful young sons, Ethan and Elijah, whose wonderment of discovery have helped me rediscover mine.

Special thanks to the Wiregrass Beekeeping Club of Southeast Alabama and especially to Roslyn Horton, Phillip Carter, and Joe Burke for their advice, support, and mentoring when it comes to honey bees.

Preface

I remember being a child and discovering for the first time there were bugs in the world that would sting. It didn't seem to matter if I was trying to rescue a wasp from a mud puddle or capturing a bumble bee with my bare hands; they defended themselves from what they determined was danger. I also remember playing with honeybees at lunch time at school, either with a Popsicle stick with sugar remnants or a drink can.

The honeybees have always fascinated me. The more I learned about them the more I was amazed as to how God had created a highly intelligent insect. I hope you too will be fascinated by the incredible honeybee and this book helps, to some extent, satisfy that fascination. Enjoy.

PART ONE – THE HONEYBEE: A SOCIAL CREATURE

Can You Sense the Spring?

Can you feel the sunlight warm, streaming through the trees?
Melting sparkling, crystal snow, breaking loose winter's freeze,
Preparing slumbering dormant buds, for springing into leaves,
Can you feel the sunlight warm, streaming through the trees?

Can you smell the flowered wind, wafting its perfume?
Lush, brilliant, meadow carpet, a rainbow now in bloom,
Swaying, budding wood, adding its flavor to the tune,
Can you smell the flowered wind, wafting its perfume?

Can you hear the honeybees, flying through the air?
Buzzing from flower to flower, with precision and great care,
Harvesting with great diligence, what the blooms have to share,
Can you hear the honeybees, flying through the air?

Can you see the butterflies, dancing on the wing?
With a graceful, melodious waltz, that nature alone can bring,
Light and lively creatures, these aerial heralders of spring,
Can you see the butterflies, dancing on the wing?

Can you taste the springtime rain, falling from the sky?
The thirsty earth does drink it in, as if its throat was dry,
Cool brooks now enlivened, give off a refreshing sigh,
Can you taste the springtime rain, falling from the sky?

So, with your senses heightened, take the springtime in,
Bees to butterflies to fragrances, lofty on the wind,
Embrace the warming rays, and dance when the rains begin,
Yes, with your senses heightened, take the springtime in.

It's a Lady's World

The worker bee is the backbone of the community. She makes up 90-99% of the bee hive depending on how many males or drones are in the colony. Let's look at her humble beginning and existence. Her life may last from six weeks to six months, depending on the season and the needs of the colony. Many bees will work themselves to death; all in the name of preserving the hive during the spring and summer harvesting season.

Like all other bees she will start out as an egg about the size of a grain of rice which is deposited by the queen in a cell in the honeycomb. The egg will grow until it becomes a larva or baby. At this time the other bees will feed her a combination of pollen and royal jelly. At the right time, the nurse bees will cut the royal jelly consumption off and continue to feed the baby just pollen. Too much royal jelly and the larva will become a queen. Too little royal jelly and the larva will become a drone. The worker-to-be is given just enough royal jelly to make her female, but her ovaries will not become developed like the queen.

The larva will grow with her head pointed toward the opening so she can be fed. She will grow several days until she fills the cell. When the bees determine the larva is old enough, they will seal the cell over with wax and let the baby continue to grow. This next growing stage is the pupa stage. The older larva will spin a cocoon inside the cell. Inside the cocoon and cell the larva will develop into a bee. At the right time she will hatch out of the cell. The whole process is similar to the process of the caterpillar turning into a butterfly.

Once the developed pupa becomes a bee she will eat her way out of the cell casing. Her first order of business is to clean the cell she just came out of to prepare it for another egg. This is a janitorial phase and once done, she will move on to the nursing stage, where she will help other nurse bees take care of the young. She can't fly just yet, so she must work inside the hive. She will help retrieve pollen from the bees as they arrive back from harvesting. The pollen is used immediately to feed the babies or is stored for later use. She will also consume honey and will secrete beeswax during this phase in order to build up the hive.

In the next phase, her wings have a greater strength and are more development, but not quite enough to allow for long flights. The stinger is developing too. At the guardian or protecting phase, the worker will stay close to the hive and still has some duties within. As she guards the hive she will continue to flex and strengthen her wings.

The last phase of worker's life is the foraging stage. In this phase, her wings are fully developed and she will leave the hive in search of nectar,

Bees foraging on waste beeswax

sugars, water, and pollen. She will travel up to two miles away to forage for these commodities for the hive. Along with her wings, her stinger is completely developed and can inflict the most pain and damage when used. Now, she will work as a scout and a forager. These duties are interchangeable. When she finds water, sugar, pollen, or nectar, she will arrive back at the hive and alert the other foragers as to what she has found and how to get there.

The worker honey bee knows her job and she does it well. All too often she will give up her life for her prime objective: preservation of the hive. Her death is often by one of two means; she either stings (where she dies from trauma) or she works herself to death. Either way, she has succeeded in why she existed.

The Queen Bee

Queen Cells on a Domestic Frame

In the hierarchy of the honey bee world there are three classes: the queen, the worker, and the drone. A trained eye can tell the difference in the three by body and wing structure. The queen is larger and longer than the general population with an extended abdomen. The drone, the male, is stubbier and has larger wings. The worker is the common bee who does all the work.

Being the queen is not as glamorous as it sounds. She is constantly at work producing eggs. She is an egg laying machine. At the peak of the egg laying season (spring time) she can lay several hundred eggs a day. At her start she was a typical egg. For some reason in the hive, it was determined a new queen was needed. Either the present queen (momma) was failing in her duties or the hive was about to swarm; these would be the most common reasons. When it is decided a new queen is needed, the worker bees begin to feed several babies an increased amount of royal jelly (a secretion from worker bees), more than the rest of the babies. These babies are in special cells called queen cells. The new queen will receive this royal jelly for her entire lifetime. Her body, unlike the rest of the female bees, develops ovaries and thereby develops into a queen. In total there are about three or four more would be contenders to the throne in the hive. The first queen to hatch will thwart any attempts by fellow queens to take over. The new queen will do this by assassinating these contender queens while they are still inside their cells by stinging them through the cell wall, eliminating any contention for her throne.

What about momma? Well, either momma will be or has been killed by the workers (yes, another assassination) or she is about to leave the hive with some of the workers and honey to start another hive. If momma is about to leave she will secrete a pheromone which tells the hive she is leaving. This signals the workers who elect to go with her to gorge themselves on honey. They will need it to build a new hive. The honey is digested by the workers and in return they secrete beeswax for building a hive in a new location.

If for some reason momma decided not to leave or was too weak to leave, her and her daughter would battle it out for the throne. More often than not, if momma was weak or wounded, the workers would converge on her (ball her up) and suffocate her. Most of the time momma leaves without confrontation. Sometimes mother and daughter will co-rule. Though it happens, this is rare.

While the new queens (the survivor and contenders) were growing in their cells, the worker bees were also growing out drones. The drones are the males. These males will contend to mate with the new queen; this is a onetime occurrence. The new queen will fly out of the hive straight up into the air. Only the fastest drones will catch up with her and mate with her. The faster males will be the strongest and a more desirable blood line.

Notice the Queen is longer than the others. Can you spot her?

When the new queen returns to the hive she will set up shop and begin laying eggs at an amazing rate. Now her abdomen is extended and in time her wings will not be used and will atrophy. She won't use her wings again until she, like her predecessor swarms from the hive. She will become so big she will not be able to feed herself; her attendants will have to do it for her. She will be a viable egg producer for about three years depending on her breed.

It would be a misnomer to say the queen is fat and happy. She is large, but this is a byproduct of her role. She, like her working counter parts, is expendable if it means keeping the hive alive. As long as she is productive and viable, she will be allowed to rule. When she starts to fail in her duties she will abdicate the throne or be removed.

The Poor Drone

The drone is the male honey bee. He is definitely not in control. It is a girl's world after all. The drones (when they are around) do not make up more than 1 to 10% of the hive. It is more like the 1% than 10. They serve one useful purpose: mating with the queen. Since the queen mates one time shortly after she assumes her throne, the drones are not needed after that. See the previous chapter "The Queen Bee" for more details. The hive decides when the males are needed. This is accomplished by the amount of or lack of royal jelly that is fed to the babies. See

A baby drone with new wings yet to unfurl

the chapter "It's a Lady's World" on page 11 for more information on how the gender is determined by the hive.

The drone is larger than the smaller worker female bee. He can be sometimes mistaken for the queen to the inexperienced bee keeper. Depending on the species he will be thin or wide, but across all breeds he will have bigger wings for two purposes; the first is so he can catch up to the queen for mating. The second purpose is for defense, since he has no stinger; his only means of any defense is his oversized wings. This gives him a sound advantage. That is, he sounds more ominous

Here are three drones that have been pushed from the hive by workers. This colony recently swarmed, at that time, the drones were needed to mate with the queen. Since that has happened, these drones are no longer needed and were pushed out to die.

than he really is and hopes to scare off any attacker with sound. When the hive is under attack they create a buzz to make it sound as if there are more bees present than there truly is, while the ladies take on the attacker through stinging.

Unlike "The Bee Movie", the drone does nothing else useful in the hive. He doesn't work. He doesn't produce honey. He doesn't produce beeswax. He doesn't collect pollen, nectar, or water. The drone hangs around the hive and smooches off the colony. He is most commonly found around the honey stores helping himself to what is there. The workers do not mind the guys hanging around, though they sometimes can be a nuisance. I know what you are thinking; "What a lazy bee." Well, as stated before, his function is strictly for the continuance of the blood line through mating with the queen. Only the strongest and fastest will mate with her; this is by design.

So why the title "Poor Drone"? These poor guys haven't got a clue. Their lives are shortened more than not by the worker bees. See, the ladies will only put up with a freeloading man for so long, and then it's out the door. In the winter when the honey stores can run low, either due to damage to the hive or a poor season of collections, someone has to go without food. It won't be the queen. It won't be the babies. It will be the drones first. The workers will prohibit the drones from entering the hive and suck up the honey reserves. They will stop them at the door and eject them from the hive. Drones are outnumbered almost 10 to 1. So they don't have a fighting chance. The workers will starve the drones to death. The starving of the drones may sound cruel. It is an unwritten rule (bees can't write) everyone must work to the goal of hive preservation even to the point of sacrifice.

What a Designer

Of all of nature's builder insects, the honey bee stands close to the top. It is a versatile little creature that is intelligent in its own right. The honey comb design, hexagonal, has been proven to be one of the most structurally sound designs known to man. This six sided design is used in such things from aircraft design to surf boards because of it space and weight saving attributes.

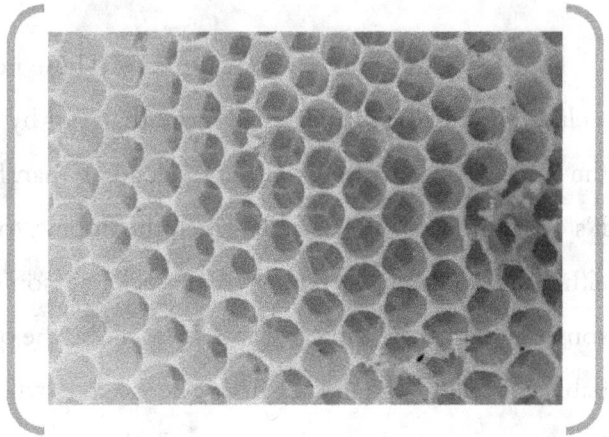

Honey bees will build almost anywhere that suits their needs. They prefer to build in a closed box type structure. I have extracted bee hives ranging from outside of a building to concrete blocks to inside a carpeted compartment in a RV camper. All the honey bee needs is a little hole to get in and out of. They favor to have more than one entrance. They will choose a site with one way in and out if that is the best they can do. Sometimes bees will reuse a home that has been vacated by another hive.

The honey bees need a place which is well ventilated. They need to control the temperature in the hive or colony and, they also need to control the amount of moisture in the honey. This is done by controlling the amount of evaporation before sealing the honey in the comb. Bees control the ventilation in the hive by two distinct ways. One way is by the flapping of their wings. It is not uncommon to see bees bearding (gathering) at the entrance of the hive. Either the hive is too hot, and they need to cool it down, or they need to

Bees bearding in the heat of summer

evaporate the water content from the honey. Two, they will seal up cracks in the hive with Propolis. Wikipedia defines Propolis as "a resinous mixture that honey bees collect from tree buds, sap flows, or other botanical sources." It has other uses by humans for health benefits as well. Yet, it works extremely well as a bee caulk.

In an attempt to control the moisture and ventilation, bees will select a location which is free from direct elements. They elect to get the moisture they need from water supplies outside their colony. That is why you will see bees at water sources like puddles, pools, ponds, etc. They are gathering water to make their honey. They will also get water from the nectar they harvest. They particularly love cola drink cans and bottles. They get an added plus: sugar and water source. Be sure in the spring and summer to check your drinks if they have been sitting awhile. You may have an unexpected visitor.

Bees build with wax which is secreted from glands on their abdomens. The bees will eat eight to ten pounds of honey to produce one pound of beeswax. They use the wax to draw out the comb and for sealant. The sealant is called capping or caps. Caps are put over completed honey and over baby bees at a particular time of their development.

Another example of bees bearding in the summer time

The honey bee is an amazing architect and builder; constructing the same designs for thousands of years. She displays simple elegance in her designs. From beautiful and sturdy structures to cross ventilation, the honey bee shows some of the best ideas can be discovered in nature.

Communicator and Navigator

The honey bee has an incredible sense of communication. There are two primary ways bees can recognize each other, their hive, and transmit information. They recognize others in their community and their hive by the smell of pheromones. These pheromones have a distinctiveness the bees smell. The other and most common way honey bees communicate is by body motion or dancing.

A Swarm of Bees Following Their Queen

Pheromones

When a colony is overcrowded or if the queen is old and no longer viable to lay eggs, the colony can sense it as does the queen. She will begin to emit a pheromone which tells the hive the queen is about to swarm. The worker bees will begin preparation for the swarm. If a colony has a weak queen they will build queen cells at the top of the hive. (See "The Queen Bee" for more on queen creation). When the colony has an overcrowding issue they will build queen cells at the bottom of the hive. When the new queen has hatched, the reigning queen will emit a pheromone indicating it is time to swarm. The swarm workers will gorge themselves on honey to use to start the new hive. When the queen's wings are strong enough for

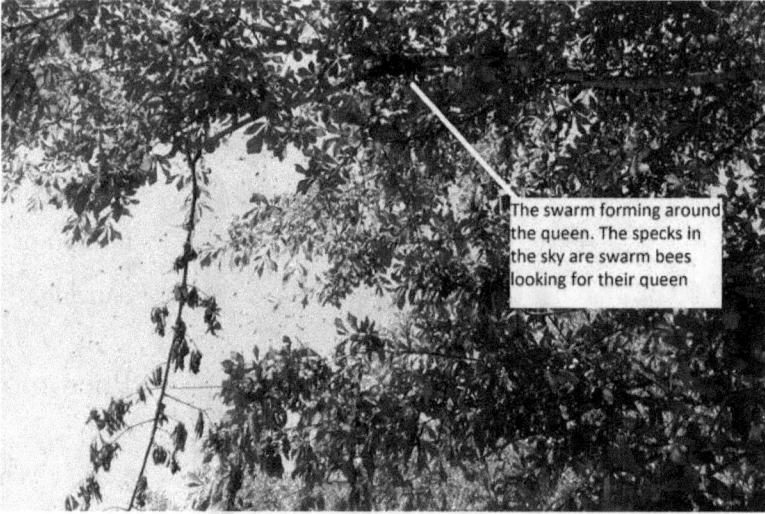

The swarm forming around the queen. The specks in the sky are swarm bees looking for their queen

flight, she will leave the hive and the swarm has begun. The swarm will look like a living cloud. The bees will fly around smelling for the queen as she flies. When she lands upon an object the bees will gather around her forming a blob of bees (See the back cover for a picture of what this can look like). The swarm may stay on the initial landing spot from twenty minutes to several days while scouts look for a suitable spot to start a new hive. Once the spot has been selected by the scouts, the queen will take flight again and the swarm will follow.

Dancing Bees

Honeybees also communicate by dancing in the hive near other bees. Specifically, scout bees will locate a commodity essential to the hive. These are nectar, sugar, pollen, and water sources. Once found the honey bee will return to the hive to tell the rest of the bees around them how to get to the source. There have been many tests to discover what the different parts of the dance (known as the waggle dance) means.

The bees will enter the hive and form a straight run then go around in circles all the while "waggling". The length of the straight run and the number of circles the bee makes communicates to the bees around her. Several studies prove bees can communicate the type, location, and distance of the commodity they have found. The straight run will tell the others the direction of the commodity and the circles will tell the distance. The length of the straight run will show the direction and the number of circles will tell how far away the source is.

In one study several plates of sugar water where placed in various locations. The scout bees were marked by the researchers with various symbols as they visited the plates. One plate was designated by a + sign and each scout was marked with a + sign. A second plate was set up and bees were marked with a -, and a third plate with a dot. When the scouts returned to the hive and danced, the researchers marked the bees in the area around the scout according to the mark on the scout. I.e. bees around the scout that had the + sign were marked with a + sign and so on. Only bees from the hive with a dot came to the plate with a dot, the ones with + to the + plate and, the - bees came to the - plate.

Honey bees navigate according to the sun. That is, they will communicate to other bees the commodity's location in proportion to the location of the sun. Similar to how we would tell someone directions to get to a someplace. I.e. "go north down the street and the store is 200 feet to the left of the post office." The post office here is like the sun and the store is the flower or water source. Bees can even navigate on a cloudy day because they use polarized light which is seen with their compound eyes.

Honey bees are also attracted to movement. This is called the "flicker effect". Bees prefer movement and complicated flower arrangements. One study showed where bees could even be trained to find food on a special card. The more complicated designs were preferred by the bees.

Honey bees are amazingly accurate in their recognition through smell and, their communication through dancing shows the highly complex, yet effective organization within their world. Just like other communities, effective communication is a key component to functionality and order; so it is in the honey bee hive as well.

Wax Maker

Beeswax is the basic building block of all honey bee hives. It is used by younger bees to build perfect comb in which honey, pollen, and babies are housed. A honey bee has two stomachs; the honey stomach and the regular stomach. The wax is a byproduct of the honey bee ingesting honey in their regular stomach. When a honey bee digests the honey it is converted into beeswax and is dispensed by a gland located in the abdomen. As the gland produces the wax in flakes, the bee works it to make the comb.

Depending on who you ask, honey bees will have to consume from 8-10 to 18-20 pounds of honey to produce one pound of beeswax. The wax will start out light in color and will darken with time as it is tainted with propolis and pollen. Refined and cleaned wax has had the propolis and pollen removed.

One pound of cleaned and refined beeswax will be worth $15 - $20 depending on the market. Beeswax, like honey bees has a long history. Egyptians used it in medicine and in mummification. It has also been used in the making of jewelry. Before there was gum to chew, children and adults alike enjoyed chewing the honeycomb.

Candles made from beeswax have been used for centuries. The Roman Catholic Church required all candles contain from 25-65% beeswax, depending on the use within the church. Beeswax candles do not produce soot like paraffin or soy candles. Beeswax candles are desirable because they are near smokeless and dripless. It has been found that when beeswax candles had been burned in churches and monasteries the wax atomized and coated paintings in the

Beeswax votive candles

buildings. In effect, the beeswax preserved the paintings over the centuries.

Beeswax is still used today in medicines, beauty products, sealants, and polishes. Medicines include lip balms and creams for skin ailments. In beauty products, it is used in lipsticks and soaps. It is also used in instrument mouthpieces called reeds. It is used in furniture and floor sealants and polishes and has been used even in toilet bowl rings. Beeswax is also used as additives in foods such as gums and candies.

The humble bee sets out to create a home for her food, stores, and babies and man has taken this great gift to enhance his life beyond the hive. Though beeswax is not a necessity of life, however, it has brought tremendous improvement to mankind's quality of life through the centuries.

A Mythical Creature

Egyptian legend relates how the honey bee was part of the creation story. According to tale, Ra the sun god cried tears of honey. When those tears hit the ground they became honey

Sumarian Bee Goddess

bees. These bees formed the first hives. Therefore, honey was considered fit only for those who were of royalty, because it was thought to be formed by the supreme god.

Honey bees were symbolic of royalty and god-likeness. For example, several gods, Vishnu, Pan, and Aphrodite, are depicted as honey bees on a flower. There were royal bee keepers whose sole existence was to provide the royalty of the nation with honey and wax. Napoleon made sure honey bees were part of his coronation robes and there were bees found woven into some of his tapestries. Pharaohs also used the honey bee as a symbol of royalty in official seals and jewelry. In the tomb of Childeric I three hundred golden honey bees were found.

Bees were thought to be a link between life and the afterlife. One Greek myth tells how the bee carried the doomed soul to Hades in the underworld. Honey was used for embalming and has been found covering the dead. Honey was found in the tomb of King Tut in a food jar. A tradition of the hill people in the American Appalachian region was to go tell the bees when someone had died in the family so the bees could spread the news.

Certain legends claim when one sees a honey bee flying; it is the fleeting of a soul of a human who has just died. If you have ever seen the Christmas Classic "It's a Wonderful Life" with Jimmy Stewart the angel Clarence explains to him every time you hear a bell sound an angel "gets his wings". Just like angels getting their wings when a bell sounds, if you die in the presence of a honey bee, it will carry your soul from this earth. So, I have to wonder, what happens if there are no bees around? Another depiction of this is in the TV show "The Ghost Whisperer." In the opening credits you can see a bee flying to a lady whose dress is made of bees. This first bee lands as part of the dress and another takes off signifying the departure of the soul.

Another folktale tells of how the patron saint of beekeepers, St. Ambrose was allegedly found by his father covered with honey bees as a baby. Later in life he would be referred to as the Honey Tongued Doctor because of his sweet preaching and speech. This goes along with the belief; if a bee lands on the lips of a child, the child will become a great speaker.

Honey bees and the colony have long been symbolic of the perfect society. Many societies use the honey bee as the natural basis for a monarchy. A hive has one ruler, the queen; though in times past the queen was mistakenly thought to be a king. This monarchy represents one ruler with many subjects working in harmony and in unison. The honey bee is oblivious to all the attention given her over the centuries and she just keeps on doing what God designed her for; the preservation of the hive and a producer of that sweet insect syrup known as honey.

A Luxury Bug

I once heard that Albert Einstein said if all the honey bees in the world were to disappear then it would be the end of mankind. Now, I am that kind of person when someone makes a statement like that, I often respond with: "And you base that on what?"

A little research will show honey bees pollenate around 80 different crops. These crops can range from fruits, like blueberries to nuts, like almonds. Notice fruits and nuts, though good and good for you, are not necessary. These are luxury crops. In fact, the food crops the honey bee pollinates are crops we can essentially do without. They do not pollenate grasses or grains like barely, wheat, corn, or millet; though they will occasionally obtain pollen from these grains. These crops would sustain us if the honey bee were to disappear, but imagine how bland oatmeal would be without honey to put on it.

The honey bee is an interesting, and I would dare say a royal creature. She is the workhorse of the flying insect world like the ant is to the crawling world. She is royal in nature due to the byproducts of her labor. What would life be like without watermelons and cantaloupes on a hot summer day? Imagine life without cherries, strawberries, pears, and apples…no apples, no apple pie. It would be un-American (for us Americans that is).

Granted, there are other insects which could pollenate these crops, like the little black bee in America who is native to the area, but not to the degree and scope as a hive of honey bees. Black bees have not had the inroads the honey bee has enjoyed and they are also very hard, if not impossible to keep in a hive. Bumble bees, though a pollinator as well, will have a hive of around one hundred ladies in the house as opposed to tens of thousands of honey bees per colony. No other bee except the honey bee exists in such a high concentration.

In the northern European countries, the honey from these regal creatures was used to make mead. Mead is a drink made from fermented honey. It is honey wine. The taste is (to me) like a combination of whisky and wine. In the northern most parts of Europe, grapes did not grow so wine could not be made. Honey bees did exist and they made honey. So the Norsemen used what they had and made their honey-wine called mead. Mead was a staple drink. You find it at the center of the tables and fables in mead halls. Remember reading Beowulf in school? Beowulf and friends were in the mead halls and they were eating and drinking mead. I wonder if they ever lifted a mug to the majestic honey bee.

KBC

Soap from beeswax

Though life would continue without the majestic honey bee, many industries would suffer and face collapse. Our lifestyle would see a drastic alteration. Luxuries we now enjoy would be gone or so expensive they would be appreciated by only the very rich. Beautiful flowers would not be as abundant and spring time would be less dramatic. So next time you see a busy honey bee conducting her daily duties, pause and thank God for His creation of this noble creature.

Defender to the End

When the honeybee decides to sting, it will mean certain death for her. Yet, she will sacrifice her life for the defense of the colony and hive. The honey bee, unlike a lot of stinging insects, cannot sting more than once. Her stinger is barbed and once imbedded into the target, will not easily come out. In fact, the stinger will be ripped out of the bee's body along with a poison sac. The sac has "muscles" if you will, that will continue to pump the bee's poison into the victim. The bee will fly or fall off the victim and will die.

Bees guarding the hive entrance. The guardians stop all intruders including other bees.

If you are stung by a honey bee, don't attempt to pull the stinger out. If you attempt to remove it with your fingers you could squeeze the poison sac and inject the rest of the poison into the site. Instead, use a credit card, a driver's license, or even your finger nail and scrape the stinger out of the skin. This scraping will effectively remove the stinger and sac without further damage. The remedy I use to alleviate some of the swelling is applying a paste made of baking soda and water to the site. When the baking soda dries and flakes off, the sting site should be less painful. Over time I have built up somewhat of immunity to the stings and it doesn't bother me as much as it might others.

If you have watched enough cartoons or Hollywood (which unmercifully picks on honey bees) you have seen the person or animal which is being attacked run like crazy, and most of the time into water to escape the bees. Bad idea. Yes, move at a swift pace, but don't run if you can help it. Bees do not like carbon dioxide. If you run then you will expel more CO_2 and thereby attract more bees. If you jump into the water, they will just wait you out. If they are on you when you jump in the water, they won't let go. If you have to run anywhere, run inside and get in a dark room with a window. The bees will go to a window to follow the natural light. Don't turn on any lights in the room; this will just let the bees see you again.

Of all the stinging insects in nature, the honey bee is one of the most docile. A bee keeper once told me the same truth applies to honey bees that apply to horses: honey bees will hurt you if they sense you are scared of them or if you disturb them. They are gentle creatures which sting out of defense. Case in point: the reason Hollywood versions of bee attacks have honey bees in them are because these bees are the easiest and safest bees to handle. If you know what you are doing, these bees can be handled in massive amounts without them stinging you. Just don't be scared of them and they won't feel threatened. That said, there are certain times of the year where honey bees will be more defensive by nature. One such season is at the end of the summer. The bees know that fall and winter is not far away. The nectar and pollen are beginning to fade and the bees know the will soon be gone. In this state, the bees are more alert to intruders and feel more threatened by visitors. However, the honey bee really gets a bad rap by Hollywood.

When the hive gets into defensive mode everyone is alerted. When one bee stings you, she will also mark you with a pheromone. This pheromone alerts the others to attack, and attack they will. They go for the face area first. Again, they are sensing the CO_2, and now they also have an additional homing signal, the pheromone from the first attacker.

In conversations regarding my extracting bee hives from buildings and such, I am asked if I get stung. I usually put it this way: the average hive contains about 30,000 to 60,000 bees. Up to 98% of those bees are females who tend the hive. Now, if you mess with the house that the wife or momma has put into order, then someone is going to pay for it. If you mess with a house that is ran by thousands of females, someone is going to pay for it. Very often, it is the one tearing up the house. Those ladies get really ticked off fast. So yes, I frequently get stung, several times. Such is the price of extracting a hive of bees.

Healthy Producer

Though honey is the main commodity bees produce, it is not the only usable product or by-product utilized by humans. Honey bees also collect pollen and store it as pre-digested food for their babies. Bees secrete a substance from a gland in their head called royal jelly which is fed to

The brown sticky stuff on top of the brood frame is propolis.

developing pupae (bee babies). They produced a caulk like substance they use to seal holes and glue parts of the hive together; this substance is called propolis. Though some of these items are discussed in other sections, let's take a closer look at what they are and what the bees and mankind has done with them over the centuries.

Honey

King Solomon stated the benefits of honey in the Bible: "My son, eat honey, for it is good and the drippings of the honeycomb are sweet to your taste." Proverbs: 24:13. Honey is the only food that does not spoil. It contains anti-bacterial and anti-fungal properties, and has been used as medicine for this reason. It also contains hydrogen peroxide. Honeys purchased in most stores have been pasteurized to keep it from crystallizing. Many unknowing people regard crystalized honey as have "gone bad." The pasteurization also kills naturally occurring enzymes. These enzymes are desirable because they are touted to have great health benefits. Further, this heat treatment also changes the taste of the honey.

Ceramic honey jar with spoon

Honey is also promoted as the perfect food which contains everything needed to sustain life. Included in the list of ingredients is water, glucose, fructose, and minerals such as iron, calcium, phosphate, sodium chlorine, potassium, and magnesium. It also contains antioxidants.

Medicinally, honey has been shown in some clinical studies, when taken internally, to alleviate or cure acid reflux, gastroenteritis, infections, sore throats, coughs, and allergies. Some believe it will also boost the immune system and give energy, promote athletic performance, weight loss, increase brain function, prevent low white blood count, and prevent cancer and heart disease. When topically applied it has been claimed to kill certain staph infections, alleviate dandruff and scalp issues, and promote healing of burns.

Bee Pollen, Royal Jelly and Propolis

Bee pollen is pollen which is collected by the honeybees as food source for the babies. The bees carry it in sacs on their legs. As with honey this pollen has been "treated" by the bees and there are assertions of health and medicinal benefits. Like honey, bee pollen is laden with minerals, vitamins, and nutrients. Bee pollen is rich in proteins, free amino acids, vitamins, including B-complex, and folic acid.

Some of the medicinal claims linked to bee pollen include: energy enhancing, skin soothing, anti-

Pollen on the hind legs of this bee. The pollen is collected from the flower and is the same color here as part of the flower.

inflammatory properties which can improve the respiratory system. Further, certain studies show bee pollen has antibiotic properties which promote blood cell health, the alieving of allergies, promotion of digestive health, boosting of the immune system, help with weight management, heart health, and stimulating and restoring ovarian functions.

The properties of royal jelly and propolis are similar to the properties of honey and bee pollen. An additional claim for royal jelly above honey and bee pollen is that it can lower blood pressure. Studies have also shown propolis to slow down cavities in teeth, remove warts, lower blood pressure, and bring relief to canker sores.

A Word of Caution

As with any medicinal or health claims, these listed here should be thoroughly researched and discussed with one's health professional before attempting to use as health aids. Further, due to the antibacterial nature of honey, it is advised not to be given to infants less than one year old as it will kill needed, good bacteria in the developing infant.

PART TWO – THE COLONY

Mixing Colonies, Cross Your Fingers

Know Your Bees

Each honey bee colony is unique. They have a personality all

their own. This personality is reflective of the queen and her children. Just about everyone in the hive is her child. If she is a new queen then the colony will eventually be her offspring since the older bees will die off. Therefore, the hive will take on the characteristics of the queen.

Bees like all other insects are divided into species. The common name of European honey bees are named after the country or region from which they originated. The different bees also have different body sizes and coloring. Cross breeding can produce results not seen in purebred bee species.

The Africanized or common named Killer Bee, is a cross breed of the Italian honey bee and the natural African honey bee. This cross production created the "Killer Bee", which cannot be identified by viewing the bee with the naked eye. The Killer Bee looks like the Italian honey bee. It has the aggressive characteristics of the African bee, yet at a higher level. The only known successful cross breeding of two species is the Italian and the African.

Species of bees are desired for the characteristics found within those strains. Italian honey bees for example are hardy bees and hard workers. They are high producers of honey and swarm less often. They can be distinguished by their light colored abdomen. Though the Italians are easy to manage, they like to rob other hives. They are very popular among American bee keepers. The German bee is a darker smaller bee. This bee is often sickly and hard to manage. The Russian bees are more disease resistant and are not prone to robbing other hives.

It is essential to know the full characteristics of your honey bees. For example, when bee keepers have to re-queen a colony; that is, replace an aging or sickly queen; it is difficult to cross some species. The Italians will sometimes take a Russian queen. As stated before the Italians will take an African queen, and the resulting bees become very aggressive and dangerous.

It is easier to specialize in care and treatment of purebred bees since the beekeeper knows what the pros and cons of each particular breed tends to be. For example, Italians tend to swarm two to three times a year in a larger number; where the Africans swarm three to four times a year. The Russians do not produce brood or babies except during the nectar flow and presence of pollen, whereas the Italian produces brood all year long.

Mixing Colonies

When mixing colonies you stand a chance of getting angry bees. These bees are very aggressive as is their queen. Some beekeepers like these aggressive bees because they are aggressive in every aspect, including the production of honey and yet, they can be hard to keep. The aggressiveness is not desired, it can be bred out of the colony by introducing a new queen. I know of some bee keepers who will extinguish the whole hive because these angry bees will attack and rob other hives. They become robbers rather than productive workers and they stress the hives they attack.

There are several processes you can use to introduce bees to each other. One method is to line the top of the open host hive with newspaper and spray it with sugar water. Place an empty super (a small box the size of the hive) on top to hold the paper. Dump your bees onto the paper and put the lid on the super. The host bees and the introduced bees will each eat through the sugar-water soaked paper, which will take several days. Ideally, by the time the bees eat through the paper they are used to each other's smell and will welcome each other. The problem with this is that if the bees eat through the paper before they have gotten to know each other, they will fight. Another method of introduction is to place window screen instead of newspaper between the open hive and the super. It can then be removed in several days. Again, you take the chance of introducing the bees to each other too soon and fights ensuing.

As stated before, colonies are as unique as the queen. When introducing colonies they may just not get along no matter how hard you try. Sometimes the introduced bees will leave the hive. Sometimes they will try to take over. The chances of this happening will be increased if you leave the introduced queen with her bees. Therefore, anytime you try to mix colonies, you must separate out the queen. It is desirable for the beekeeper to kill the queen because she serves no further purpose. To leave her in the mix is to invite trouble.

There are several reasons why one would want to mix hives. These include introducing a swarm hive to an existing hive, to combine two weaker hives, or to introduce one weaker hive to a stronger one. Just remember personalities of hives play a large part in mixing colonies. The most successful mixes come when the same breeds are mixed (i.e. Italian bees with Italian bees). Both colonies are more apt to accept each other and live in harmony to produce a stronger and healthier hive. There are no guarantees with the mixing of hives, but if done successfully you will have one stronger hive.

Unwelcomed Guests

You find honey bees in your wall or in your shed or even in the space between the floors of your home. Now what? They can't stay there. Even if you are a friend of nature, it is hard to share your abode with thousands of buzzing and, sometimes stinging honey bees.

There are a few things you should know about your new guests. Though it may look as if your honey bees have damaged your home, it is frequently quite the opposite. The bees find existing damage where there is a hole and then they move in. For instance, squirrels are notorious for chewing on eaves and soffits of homes. If this constant chewing creates a hole in your soffit and scout bees find it, there is a possibility of the bees moving in.

Once inside a cavity in a building, honey bees will begin to construct their comb to store honey, pollen, and their young. They will even water proof the cavity and stop up other holes so they can control how much air flow is allowed in the hive. They will do their best to fill the cavity with as much comb as possible during the spring and summer season in preparation for the winter.

In older homes honey bees prefer un-insulated walls. These walls will sometimes have knot holes that allow the honey bees easy access. The older walls provide a nice 2 x 4 to 6 inch cavity to construct a fine bee home. It is even better if no humans are living in the home. This allows the bees to multiply undetected and undisturbed. I have seen bees build a large hive in the spaces between floors in occupied two-story homes. The bees have somehow gained access and now they have a tunnel the width of the home. Most ceiling/ floor spaces are 2 feet wide by up to 10" or even 12" high. This makes for a large box for the colony to live in. I once removed such a hive. It was so deep into the ceiling/ floor space that I had to use a scrapper with a handle five feet long to reach the entire honeycomb.

So you decided to have the hive removed. I concur. To try to exterminate the hive will often take several attempts by a pest control company; even then it may not be successful. The pesticide spray will may kill the bees closest to the hive opening, while the queen will hide and will be unaffected. You will see diminished activity for a while. When a new crop of bees hatch out and begin flying, many people think the bees are back, when in reality, the bees never left.

Let's say the exterminator was successful in killing the hive. Now there are no more bees and there is no one to tend to the hive. The dead bees will begin to rot. The unattended babies and eggs will die and also rot. The honey will become contaminated and then begin to spoil and run. The proof that the dead hive is now rotting is evidenced by the stench of thousands of dead bees and, the presence of a black goop oozing through your ceiling and/or wall. Now you will have to have the hive removed in a rotten state and have the damage repaired. This is why I always recommend total removal of the hive: queen, workers, comb, and honey.

Who will remove the hive? If you are adventurous you can do it yourself. Most home owners are not so daring. The best place to start will be with your local agricultural extension agent. Chances are very good he or she knows someone reputable to remove the hive. Know who you are dealing with:

- Check the credentials of anyone claiming to know how to remove the hive. Get references.

- How many hives have they removed in the past? You want experience.

- Do they charge? You might be able to get someone to do it for free, but remember you get what you pay for. If you want better chances of it done right, go with a professional.

- Get an estimate and get it in writing. It would be better to get a low to high range price. No one knows what is behind the wall or ceiling until part of it is removed. When I removed hives I preferred to give the home owner a low price up to what I think it will cost, in a best to worst case scenario. Rarely, did I charge the higher price.

- Do you need someone to repair the house or is repairing the damage part of the bee removal?

- Is the work guaranteed? Again, get it in writing. I guaranteed my work for at least one year after the extraction if I did the repair work. I could not guarantee bees will stay out if someone else did the repair.

- Beware of anyone wanting money up front. I invoiced all my clients. I would suggest not paying until the work is complete.

- Take time to talk with the removal expert. Treat them as any other contractor. Have them explain what they are going to do and how long it will take.

- Be open-minded. Don't shy away from a removal expert just because he says he "doesn't know" when asked a question. He may not know until he opens up the structure. However, if you have the right to get another opinion.

- Settle on what will be done with the demolition debris and what will be done with the honey, bees, and waste. Many times the removal expert will want to keep the honey and sell it to help offset the cost. I did this and estimated the job cheaper if there was a lot of honey recovered.

- Negotiate. The more the bee removal expert has to do, the more he will charge. If there are repairs or clean up you could do, this might save you some money. I gave a discount when I didn't have to clean up a mess. For example, if I am tearing off siding to retrieve bees and the home owner is going to replace it anyway, then I wouldn't charge as much.

- If you have children, ask the bee removal expert to try to explain as much as possible to them. This is a wonderful learning experience. I often took pictures of the hive and also gave some of the honey comb to the family. It helped them experience nature and the beauty of honey bees.

Remember, no two hive situations will be the same and no two bee hive removal specialists do the removal the same. Again, start with your agricultural extension agent, or you can contact a local beekeeper, or beekeeping club, to recommend someone to you to remove the hive. One last note: not all hives can be removed. When this is the case, it will have to be destroyed in place. Unfortunately, the homeowner will have to deal with the remnants of the dead hive.

A Colony Removal

As helpful as honey bees are to our way of life, sometimes they become a nuisance. The problem occurs when a swarm queen and her followers take up

residence in someone else's residence or business. The conversation normally starts with the owner stating they are finding dead honey bees in their building. Most of the time the building in question is a house, though I have seen and removed hives from wooden structures, block buildings, sheds, and even RV campers. The hive in the camper I removed was the only hive I have extracted that was living in a room with carpet. The bees had set up shop in the compartment that housed the power cord to the RV in the master bed room. The bottom of the compartment was lined with carpet. This colony was really living in style, but I digress.

There are a few questions I will ask the caller.

"Are you sure they are honeybees?" I have been told "Yes" to find out when I get there the pests are yellow jackets or hornets.

"How do you know they are honey bees?" Most of the time, the caller does not know. Evidence of honey dripping down a wall is a good sign or a bad sign; depending on how you look at it. Just because intruders may "look like honey bees" is not concrete proof. There are several bees, wasps, and hornets that could pass for honey bees to the unaware viewer.

"What kind of building are they in?" Honey bees prefer to be in an exterior wall though I have removed them from the spacing between floors. Even when this was the case, they were still towards the outside wall. If someone tells me they are in the attic or in the

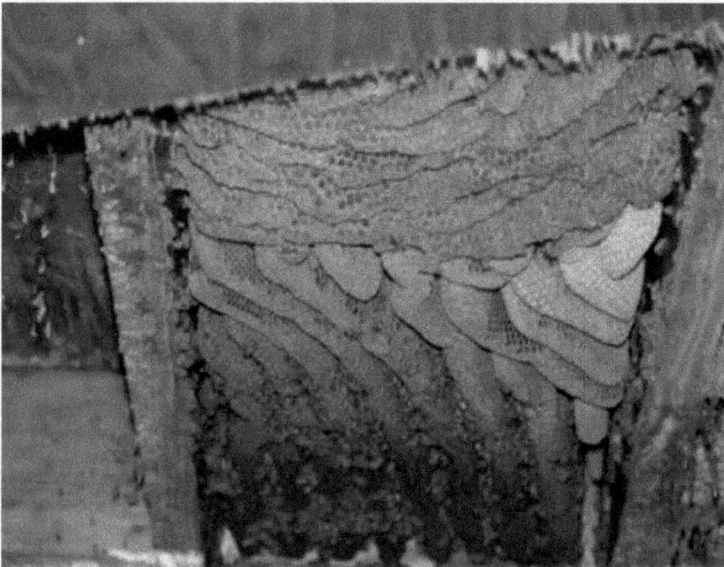

Bees in Space Between Floors in Two Story House

basement or under the house, I am somewhat skeptical. Again, there are exceptions; I once found a hive under a house.

When satisfied that I may indeed have an active bee colony, I will arrange for a free estimate. Yes, I do charge to remove honey bees. Some people think the honey and the bees I retrieve should be payment enough. I am not the one with the bee problem. I am the one with the knowledge and the bee equipment to extract the problem. The price of the honey (if it is useable), the beeswax, and what bees I save are not enough to offset the cost of my time and activity. That's just business. Also, I guarantee my work. That is, I guarantee bees will not be back within a year, if I do the repairs to the structure. Proper repair and sealing of the building should keep another colony from taking up residence. If bees do return, I will remove the new bees and do all subsequent repairs free of charge.

So we have an active honey bee colony. What now? Let's say it is in an exterior wall. After assessing the situation; I decide how to remove either the interior or exterior wall facing to access the hive. The set-up is based on the tools I need which can range from a bucket truck to scaffold to a ladder. I estimate the time it will take to remove the hive and how many helpers I will need, I have to pay them. I will give a basic estimate to the home owner of the cost of removal and repair of the structure. The estimate will run from the lowest cost to the highest. After all, we really do not know what we have until we remove the wall facing; then it's too late to negotiate with thousands of bees buzzing around. In most cases, I have charged the owner less than the higher amount estimated. It has been a rare and an extreme instance when I have had to charge more for the work.

Once we don our protective gear we will force smoke into the hive. This does two things: it will dull the bees' senses and it will fool the bees into thinking there is a fire. The dulling of the senses makes it harder for the bees to find you. When one does locate you and decides to sting, she will mark you so the others can find you too. With dulled senses it is harder for them to locate you. The bees, thinking there is a fire will rush to the honey stores, where they will gorge themselves in preparation to evacuate the hive. This way they will have honey to start another colony should they leave this hive.

With a special bee vacuum or bee-vac, I remove as many bees as possible into a holding cage by sucking them up. This cage is designed to hold the bees without hurting them. As you may guess, not everyone makes the rough trip into the cage without damage, especially the fragile queen. She rarely can handle the abuse, but most workers will do well.

The honeycomb is removed with a scraper and placed in a bucket or pan. The bees are sucked off the comb before the comb is placed in the bucket. The comb is separated into two buckets or pans. One pan will hold honeycomb and the other will hold brood, (ones with eggs) and pollen. I don't want to mix these up since I am trying to save the honey as well. Both sets of comb will be put into a freezer. This will kill pests such as small hive beetles and any other honey bees. This is quick and painless to the bees.

Once the entire comb and the majority of the bees have been removed, it is time to clean up and seal the wall back. The cavity is dusted with a slow acting poison and the remaining bees are sprayed with pesticide. As much as I would love to save every bee, it is not practical to do so; some will have to be killed. The majority will be taken alive.

Depending on the size of the hive and location, the decision may be to let it air out before sealing it back up. When the former hive area is ready to be sealed, whatever removed materials will need to be put back in place. All entrances to the former hive will be sealed and the finish/repair, if done right, will look like there was never a hive present in the first place.

It is desirable and noble for one to attempt to keep the bees who have survived the vacuuming. As stated in the chapter on mixing colonies, this is not always possible.

A Colony Removal in Pictures

Accessing where the bee colony is located. Here they are in the wall in the second story and in the space between floors.

Quick Facts

> Honey is the only food that does not spoil and is the only food produced by an insect which is eaten by mankind.

> Bees communicate by pheromones and dancing, mainly through the waggle dance.

> A honeybee's brain is oval in shape and about the size of a sesame seed. It is proportionately bigger than most insects.

> Worker bees are always female.

> Honey bees are not native to North America.

> To keep warm in the winter bees will create a ball. The inside of the ball has been measured as high as 93° F.

> There are 10 different varieties of honeybees and only one successful, long term cross breed – Africanized or Killer Bees.

> Where most honeybees will attack an intruder a few at a time, the Africanized colony will attack in force. Unleashing the entire colony if necessary to stop the intruder.

> Bee communities are called colonies or swarms. The hive is their home.

> A strong colony of bees will have on average of 40,000 to 60,000 bees.

> The average colony will travel about 90,000 miles to make 1 kg (a little over 2 pounds) of honey. That is equivalent to three trips around the world.

- Colonies will collect up to 66 lbs. of pollen each year.

- Each honeybee colony has its own distinct smell. This is how bees can tell their hive from others in the bee yard.

- Honeybees can emit up to six different pheromones to communicate. Each meaning something different to the colony.

- The Hollywood version of a honeybee hive is incorrect. What is passed off as a hive for honey bees is more like a hornet's nest.

- Beekeepers are apiarists and their bee yard is an apiary. Medicinal use of honey and other bee products is known as apitherapy.

- The term honeymoon comes from the Norse tradition of drinking honey wine (mead) for a month after a wedding.

- Honeybees can fly up to 15 mph.

Bee with pollen on back leg

- The honeybee's wing flaps at the rate of about 200 beats per second.

- One honeybee worker can produce up to 1/12 of a teaspoon of honey in her lifetime.

➢ The queen is the only bee in the colony that has a stinger without a barb on it. She does not use it for defense. The only time she will use it is shortly after she is born and then to take out fellow queens.

➢ Honeybees never sleep.

➢ The queen honeybee can lay between 1500-2500 eggs a day and up to 1 million in her lifetime, which can be about 5 years.

➢ Bees will fly up to 2-3 miles from the hive for water, nectar or pollen.

➢ Foraging honeybees can visit up to 2000 flowers a day.

This bee is collecting water

➢ Honeybees pollinate over 80% of all crops in the U.S.

➢ Honey was found in a clay jar in King Tut's tomb. Believed to be over 2500 years old and it was still good.

➢ They do not like carbon dioxide.

➢ Honeybees do not like fabric made from animal fur such as wool. They do like light color fabric made from plants such as cotton.

- They are the only bees which die after they sting.

- Honeybees have hair on their five eyes; two large eyes on the side and three in the center. They are compound eyes that can see polarized light.

- Honeybees cannot see the color red. They do not like dark colors. They see white, yellows and light blues as friendly.

Several eyes can be seen here

- Honey is the only food source containing everything needed to sustain life including water.

- Honey is made up of 80% sugars and 20% water.

- Honey bees can disconnect their wings from their muscles. They pump these muscles to create heat.

- One ounce of honey is enough fuel for a honeybee to fly around the world.

- A honeybee has two stomachs; one for eating and one for storing nectar. This one is referred to as the honey stomach.

- Honey is anti-bacterial and contains hydrogen peroxide.

PART THREE – KEEPING BEES

The equipment for bee keeping can be broken down into two parts: equipment for the bees and equipment for the keeper. The equipment for the bees consists of the hive and all its parts, and the equipment for the keeper consists of protective equipment and tools.

The Bees' Equipment

Top view of frames in a brood box

The hive is the house for the bees. The colony is housed inside the hive. A collection of rouge or homeless bees (though temporary) is referred to as a swarm. Though there are variations among keepers as to what parts of the hive will be used according to personal preference and/or location, there are basic parts that all agree on. These are the bottom board, the brood box, the super(s), the top, and the frames. Additional parts may include a hive stand, a queen excluder, and an inner board. Most all of these parts are made from wood that is not treated. This wood is finished according to the keeper's preference. Most keepers will paint the hive with a light color of water based exterior paint.

As shown in the illustration at the end of this section, the board is the foundation of the hive. Most bottom assemblies are solid and made of wood. To control various pests, such as mites, the keeper will sometimes replace this board with a screened opening.

The next box shown in the illustration is the brood box which houses the bulk of the workers, babies, and the queen. The brood box is approximately 20 inches long by 15 inches wide and 9 ½ inches high. Frames specifically designed to fit here are laid in the box for the bees to draw out into cells for the queen to lay her eggs, the young to be raised, and pollen food

KBC

Metal Queen Excluder

source to be stored. Nine to ten frames are inserted in each box. Some colonies will be so large that there is the need for two brood boxes; one stacked on top of the other. If the keeper elects to use a queen excluder it will be placed on top of the brooding area. Honey stored in the brood area will be used to sustain the colony through the winter.

The queen excluder is a thin slotted platform which has slits in it big enough for workers to pass, but not the queen; hence the name. These are made with metal or plastic. The design is to keep the queen in the brood area and out of the supers. If she is allowed into the super area she will lay eggs there and the honey will not be usable.

On top of the brood box is the first super. The super is placed on top of the excluder, if an excluder is used. Each super houses nine to ten frames designed to house just honey. As these fill up, more supers and

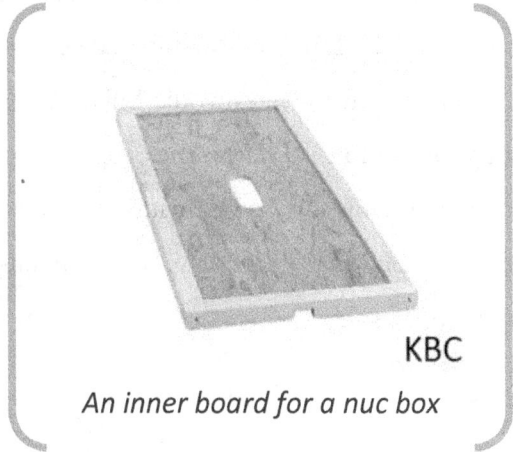

KBC

An inner board for a nuc box

empty frames are added to the stack. This honey is what is harvested from the hive. The top or cover slides over the super to keep out the elements. Some beekeepers will place an inner board inside the top super before the cover is placed. The inner cover is to keep out drafts and to keep the hive warm. In some regions the hives are plagued by the small hive beetle and the inner board gives the beetle a perfect place to hide. For this reason, I do not use an inner board. (A nuc box has about four frames and is used for starting a hive).

The frames are often made of wood and come either preassembled or assembled by the keeper. They contain thin sheets of pressed

wax as a foundation for the bees to start their process of drawing out the comb. The foundation is shaped across the surface in similar fashion of what the bees would build. As they build upon this they bring the comb cells out to the proper length to house babies, pollen and honey. This is called drawing out the comb. When these are emptied, such as in extracting, what remains is referred to as "drawn comb".

A sugar feeder supporting a captured swarm

Super

Top Cover

Queen
Excluder

Brood Box

Bottom Board

Basic Honeybee Hive with bottom board, brood box, queen excluder, one super and top cover.

The Keeper's Equipment

The keeper's basic equipment consists of head and torso protection, hand protection, a smoker, an igniter, smoker fuel, and a hive tool. Additional equipment may consist of a frame tool, honey extractor, cap removing tool such as a knife or scratcher, buckets, and large pans. As with the hive equipment, there are many more items that can fit the keeper's fancy.

There are as many different designs for head and torso selections as there are ideas. The idea is to keep the bees at bay and cover any possible exposed skin.

KBC

Pullover Veil/Hood and Shirt

The keeper needs to have a veil which covers his head and this is either tucked under the collar of a long sleeve, white or light colored

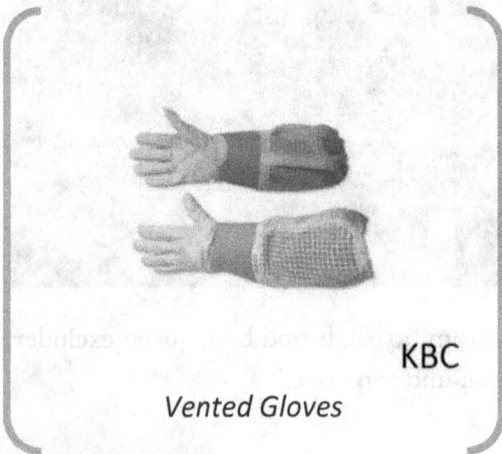

KBC

Vented Gloves

cotton shirt. The keeper may elect to use a complete upper body hat, veil, and shirt combo, referred to as the European model or a total jumpsuit. If the veil or upper body system is used, be sure to have long pants and boots.

Hand protection can range from thick poly gloves to custom purchased bee keeper leather gloves. Thin vinyl and leather work gloves will not fare well against bee stings. Depending on preference, the gloves can be tucked under the shirt sleeve or over. Either way there must be a method to stop the bees from entering into the gloves.

Most modern smokers have a protective cage around the fire pot to protect against burns. This older version still works well.

The smoker serves two purposes. The smoke from the

KBC

billowed spout tells the bees there is a fire close by and they will retreat into the hive. Some say it calms the bees, I don't really see this. It seems to alarm them. The second use for smoke is to throw off the bees' senses. When one bee stings you it will secrete a pheromone which alerts the other bees. Plus the bees do not like carbon dioxide, which you are exhaling. The smoke skews their senses and it is harder for the bees to find you. You don't need a lot when working a calm hive.

The ignitor, as it name implies is to ignite whatever fuel is in the smoker. I use grass and pine straw. It smolders well and stays lit at the bottom of the smoker. You stuff the fuel into the smoker forming a hole in the middle. Turn the smoker sideways and light the fuel at the bottom of the smoker.

When the flame is burning well, turn the smoker straight up, close the lid, and stoke the flames by pressing the bellows. Do not blow it so hard that your flame goes out. When it is established, you can gently blow smoke at the hive entrance and over the hive top once you remove the cover.

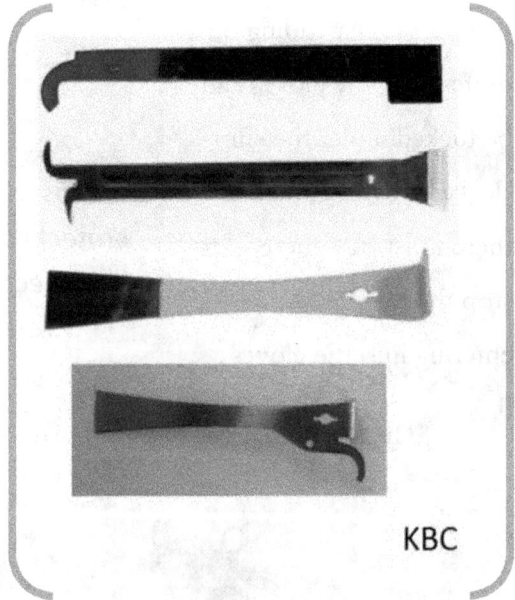

KBC

The hive tool is a flat bar or flat pry bar. It is used to pry the cover loose from the propolis the bees used to secure the lid. It is also used to pry loose the frame ends. Obviously it has many more uses, but these are the basic.

The frame tool is used to grasp the loose frames to handle them. The extractor is just that; it is used to extract the honey from the comb built into the frame. The wax knife or scratcher is used to remove the cappings of wax from the honey comb cells to release the honey. As you would imagine the buckets and pans are used for storage and transport of honey, frames, equipment, etc.

This is just the basics on equipment that a bee keeper will use to keep hives. The methods that one would prefer will tend to determine the extent of tools used. Some setups can be very elaborate.

SUMMARY

As you can imagine there is a large body of information that we have not covered in this book. We didn't touch on the types of diseases or pests that plague the honeybee. There is also the Colony Collapse Disorder that seems to be prevalent in bee circles. There are other beekeeping items that one needs to explore, such as: re-queening, state registration, capturing swarms, honey harvesting, honey extracting, winter feeding, etc.

Even still, I hope this reference guide has given you a taste of the honey bee world, a greater appreciation for the intelligent bug that God has created, and a great sense of satisfaction when you have the pleasure to taste unprocessed honey.

For more information see our bibliography, visit several websites, and locate your local beekeeping club. I would also be glad for you to reach out to me, especially if you are researching honey bees for a class project. I would love to hear from you. Our website and email is in the front of the book and on the back cover. Thank you for your interest and for reading this book.

Frames from a hive filled with honey and capped.

Picture from one of many colony removals.

BIBLIOGRAPHY

"Back Yard Beekeepers Association Website." Accessed January 24, 2015. http://www.backyardbeekeepers.com/facts.html

"Benefits of Honey Website." Accessed January 24, 2015. http://www.benefits-of-honey.com/

Bolen, John, Fr. "The Wax Candle in Liturgy." Catholicculture.org website, accessed August 29, 2015. http://www.Catholic culture.org/culture/library/view.cfm?id=6206

Borreli, Lizette. "Liquid Gold: 7 Health Benefits Of Honey That Could Heal Your Whole Body." *Medical Daily*. March 17, 2015. Accessed May 4, 2015. http://www.medicaldaily.com/ liquid-gold-7-health-benefits-honey-could-heal-your-whole-body-325932

Devito, Dominique, *Beekeeping: A Primer on Starting and Keeping a Hive* (New York: Sterling Publishing, 2010).

"Kelley Beekeeping Website." Accessed May 10, 2015. https://www.kelleybees.com/

"National Honey Board Website." Accessed January 23, 2015. http://www.honey.com/

Ohio State University, The: College of Food, Agricultural, and Environmental Sciences Website. "Bee Lab." Accessed June 20, 2011; July 21, 2015. http://u.osu.edu/beelab/

"The Bee-Chronicles Website." Accessed January 24, 2015. http://www.bee-magic.com/index.aspx

The Holy Bible, English Standard Version (ESV). (Wheaton: Crossways, 2001)

University of Florida: Institute of Food and Agricultural Sciences Extension Website. "Honey Bee Research & Extension Lab." Accessed May 12, 2011; August 2, 2015. http://entnemdept. ufl.edu/honeybee/extension/bee_college.shtml

University of Georgia Extension Website. "Bees and Beekeeping." Accessed June 15, 2011. http://extension.uga.edu/publications /detail.cfm?number=B1045

Wikipedia, The Free Encyclopedia, "Propolis." Accessed March 10, 2014. https://en.wikipedia.org/wiki/Propolis.

"www.buzzaboutbees.net website." Accessed January 23, 2015. http://www.buzzaboutbees.net/

A FREE GIFT

As a thank you for purchasing this book, we would like to send you a special gift. Using your smartphone, scan the QR code below, or on the back of the book, or go to our website at www.thehoneybeebook.info. Click on the "Contact and Purchase" tab and it will bring you to the contact page of our website. Fill out the contact info and in the "Message box" write: "Please send me my free gift" and be sure to include your mailing address.

We would have provided the free gift along with the book, but it isn't possible to attach the gift to the order of the book. We would also love to hear your comments and questions. Thanks.